G000145567

EVERY SIX SECONDS
Lighthouse Women's Aid

EVERY SiX SECONDS

A WOMAN CRiES

Published in 2011
by Lighthouse Women's Aid Ltd
Westgate House
Museum Street
Ipswich IP1 1HQ
Suffolk UK

Printed by Leiston Press.
Unit 1B
Masterlord Industrial Estate
Leiston IP16 4JD
Suffolk UK

Copyright © Lighthouse Women's Aid 2011

ISBN
978-1-907938-25-2
This book is published
with financial assistance from
Legal & General

Cover design and layout by Katy Cadwallader

Cover photograph of hourglass: Corey Amaro
http://www.willows95988.typepad.com

Inside photography by Kevin Taylor
www.kptphotography.co.uk

*As a wedding photographer, I'm used to capturing
the most joyous of occasions, so when I was asked
by Women's Aid to photograph some T shirts made
by the women they support I approached the
project with some trepidation.
What I photographed that day touched me deeply,
especially the children's clothes. I saw the whole
spectrum of human emotion laid out before me:
from despair and horror to optimism and release.
It was an honour to be involved in the project and
I wish you all good luck with the book.*
Kevin Taylor

Printed in Great Britain.

ACKNOWLEDGEMENTS

Lighthouse Women's Aid would like to thank all the supporters of this book. In particular, Sally Dynevor and Jo Brand for writing the forewords.

A special thank you to Pat Dowding and Anne Walton who guided the women through expressing themselves so eloquently, and without whom the creative writing group would not have taken place. Thank you to all the other Soroptimists and particularly to Gill Smith, who has been a support to the women when they felt they couldn't continue.

A big thank you to Legal and General for the financial support to make this book a reality and who kindly funded the first run of copies. Further thanks to Susanna Mansukhani for making this happen.

Thanks go to our CEO Sally Winston, who, when I proposed the idea, saw the potential benefits of a book like this for both the women writing, the people reading and the charity about which we are all so passionate. And to the staff of Lighthouse Women's Aid, in particular Katy Cadwallader, who has designed and laid out the book and been so patient when ideas have been changed.

But most of all, thank you to all the women and children who have contributed, and have been so candid and open about their feelings. Thanks to the women who wrote from their hearts.

And finally, thank YOU for buying a copy of this book. All proceeds are going towards providing more therapeutic services to help women and children survive the trauma of domestic abuse.

Jacqui Worbey
Community Services Manager at LWA — and survivor.

for the survivors
and those who couldn't

*"every six seconds a woman cries,
and every three days a woman dies"*

CONTENTS

Part II : The Breakthrough

Part III : The Beginning

INTRODUCTION

Ipswich Soroptimists work in a number of ways to assist the women who come to Lighthouse Women's Aid when they have nowhere else to turn to, many having put up with abuse for years. Some actions are assisting with basic needs such as providing bags with toiletries; others work in tandem with Lighthouse's own programmes designed to provide the women with practical and emotional support to give them the confidence, knowledge and skills to rebuild their lives.
Art and writing are recognized as therapeutic means of assisting people to deal with their pain and BAD experiences.

Lighthouse asked Ipswich Soroptimists to help undertake an Art project, 'The Clothes Line', where some of the women expressed their feelings and emotions in a creative way by painting on T shirts and jeans. This was very successful, as you will see from those that are included in this book to complement the poetry and personal stories. Out of this Art project came the idea of the Writing project, 'Women Write', to enable the women to release their feelings through words. It soon became apparent that their stories were ones that should be read by every woman, especially those entering a new relationship, finding themselves in a violent or abusive relationship and all men and women of goodwill who want these vicious practices to end. The idea of the book was born, its aims being to raise awareness of domestic violence and abuse.

First of all, we must pay tribute to the women who took part in this 'Women Write' project and who put their trust in two other women, both Soroptimists, most of them had never met before, and believed us when we said, 'If you can talk, you can write' – and they did – to our amazement and admiration!

We present here the outcome from seven, approximately two-hour sessions, in which we talked, cried, supported each other and wrote. Some of the group's older, unacknowledged work was brought to light and new work was produced between meetings. For some, their writing reveals a journey from despair to a feeling close to hope.

Others have not yet finished this journey but we trust that, with their newly found confidence in themselves, they will continue to believe that a good outcome is possible.

We warmly thank Jacqui Worbey and the staff at the Lighthouse Women's Aid Drop-In Centre in Ipswich for providing accommodation, all other facilities and backup where necessary. In particular we would like to thank Katy Cadwallader of Lighthouse who took our manuscript and undertook the production and design of the book as it is published. Also many thanks to Claire, one of the contributors, who helped with the typing. Not least, we are grateful to our fellow members of the Ipswich Soroptimist Club for their support, for us, and for the group's activities.

The project followed or ran in parallel with other courses or assistance which individuals received from Lighthouse Women's Aid and, for some, major life events, such as moving to a new home, took place at that time and may have had an impact on the writing.

The 'Women Write' project has proved so popular that, if the demand continues, we will repeat it. One measure of success is that one contributor has already enrolled on a degree course in English Literature and another is studying GCSE English.

Meanwhile, we commend our first venture to you in the hope that you will respond to the sufferings, hopes and fears of these brave women and work towards the elimination of such violence and abuse in our society. All profits will go to Lighthouse Women's Aid.

As one of the members of the group wrote:

I joined this writing group not being sure what to expect.
What I found was:
People that understood
People that care
And people that did not judge
You realise you are not alone
That other people have been through this.
What I found, was friends.

Pat Dowding and Anne Walton
Facilitators and Editors
Ipswich Soroptimists

JO BRAND

Violence towards women has a long history and the evidence is clear that domestic cruelty is not consigned to 'history' – it occurs in the lives of women with frightening regularity and even less widely known, to the children, male partners and husbands.

Lighthouse Women's Aid took a brave step to invite women and children, all victims of domestic abuse, to put aside their physical pain and dig deep into their battered thoughts and feelings, considerably more painful than healing bruises. Confronting humiliation, shame and degradation, lifting a pen to state clearly on paper is a brave act which the women have achieved in *Every Six Seconds*.

I would like to commend this project and thank all the contributors to Lighthouse Women's Aid for their trust and conviction that we, their readers, will strive with them to challenge domestic abuse and open 'the violence behind a closed door'.

SALLY DYNEVOR

Although I have not been affected by domestic violence on a personal level, after reading *Every Six Seconds* I feel this book will help women who are in a similar position to realise that support is out there. It is not your fault and more importantly, you can do something about it.

The proceeds of this book will go towards helping Lighthouse Women's Aid, who help women to escape domestic violence and move on to a happier, safer and stronger future. You are not alone.

Sally Dynevor
(Sally Webster in *Coronation Street*)

EVERY SiX SECONDS

PART I
The End

My Worth

It's my heart that you misuse,
And my body that you abuse,

It's my worth you don't recognise,
And my life you jeopardise,

Every six seconds a woman cries,
And every three days a woman dies,

I thank my Safety Worker for her continued support,
And the Freedom Programme for all the valuable lessons
taught,

No longer will I be the possession of a violent man,
For I'm free to choose my own destiny, define who I am.

Julie

Because He Loved Me

Because he loved me I felt special

Because he loved me I felt needed

Because he loved me I felt wanted

Because he loved me I felt protected from everything else

But it was because he loved me he had to control me

It was because he loved me he had to hurt me

It was because he loved me I didn't know who I was any
more

And it was because I loved him that I let him

Anna

All is Quiet for Now

I have tried to apologise to Bob. This is never good enough. Bob thinks that I am getting away with what I have done and will just do it again.

Nothing really changes. Wish it would.

All is quiet for now

Who is going to cook the dinner? As the problem is over me getting Bob the wrong food from a takeaway – bacon in a French stick, it should have been a baguette.

All is still quiet for now

Bob is cooking some fish and Paul (my son) is going to get some chips

All is quiet for now

Had dinner. Bob sat on his own. I said 'thank you' and went to get his plate. He told me not to. He didn't want me to do anything for him. Says he will give me something to eat I do not like, when I am hungry.

All is quiet

Bob has come up but not spoken to me. Paul is making me tea and has let Henry (the dog) out in the garden. I am going to see Toni, my next door neighbour who needs my help. Is this OK? Bob will say either 'Don't care' or something else

— he thinks I care too much about Toni and not enough about him.

I get back and Paul has gone to bed at 10pm. Bob will shout at me. He's already said he is not sleeping with me tonight – I kept him awake the night before with my snoring.

All is quiet for now

I wake up and it is next day. Who is going to get the shopping? I will ask later. Paul has asked him for me and I will go shopping and take Henry for a walk.
I went downstairs and washed and made myself some tea. Bob said that I could stay up here (in the spare room) forever and that we cannot be together. One day he is going to leave me. He says this a lot. We are still here. Nothing has changed. He says I make mistakes all the time.

All is quiet for now

Bob is making dinner. He doesn't want to give in this time. He's teaching me a lesson. I'm going down to see if he will listen and forgive me. Tell him that I am sorry again and I will be more thoughtful from now on. See what happens. He thinks I should stay in the bedroom for 2 days and saying sorry does not mean anything. He does not love me that much. I must not upset Bob any more.

All is quiet for now

Friends come round and I come down. We all talk together. Bob has been nice to me. They leave. Bob keeps on at me about what I have done wrong. He doesn't like it when I talk; he doesn't like it when I keep quiet. He says I like it all my own way; that I only do things for him to make myself feel better. Bob likes to be in control of situations. He just wants to get stoned or drunk all the time. His way of escaping. He's depressed.

When something goes wrong the day is spoilt. I don't want to do anything as everything I say or do is wrong. He is not easy to please. I don't want to start an argument.

All is quiet for now

He threatens to throw his dinner at me. He calls me a fat pig, says he is leaving. The argument gets heated, spills out on to the street. I am scared.

I did some ironing but Bob doesn't like me doing it in the kitchen.

Say sorry first, with no excuses. Take the blame.

Listen to what Bob has to say. Just wait for Bob to talk and be nice again. I do love you and don't like hurting you.

All is quiet for now

It's all my fault – not recognising the abuse for what it is.

Paula

I don't want the world to see me

I don't want the world to see me
Because I don't think they'd understand
When everything in my world is broken
I just want to know who I am

You can't fight the tears that are coming
Or the moment of truth in his lies
When everything feels like the movies
You want to bleed just to know you're alive!

Katy

Zip it bitch.
I had loved him.
Fear, shame, confused, pain.
It can't be happening to me.
My guilt. Why did I not speak out?

*The only impression he left on me
was his size 9.*

For My Husband

Life was always tough
But now it's even harder
Married to a bully
A woman beater
Remind you of your father?

A coldness that runs deep
And creeps in darkness
To the core of your soul
Bitter and twisted with a vengeance
Stripped of humanity
Eating you whole

And every day is a struggle
Just to survive
While I become a statistic
Of domestic violence
The abusers multiply
And thrive

As mothers we protect our children
From the suffering we endure
Broken and beaten
Tear-stained covered bruises
We hide the truth
The violence
Behind a closed door

No future echoes
Sound like a siren in my head
Will this death sentence be over
When enough blood is shed?

Julie

Addiction

Melancholy ran through my veins and fear had hold of my heart. I was numb. I was depressed but I couldn't leave.

I've never smoked, I hardly drink. I've never tried drugs. I don't even drink tea or coffee and although I like chocolate, I could live without it. I've never had any of the usual vices but I have had an addiction.

I was addicted to him. And like all good vices, you know in the end it's going to kill you. No matter how bad it is for you, you just can't give it up. And that's what it was like. No matter how bad he treated me, no matter how bad I felt, I couldn't stop it.

Anna

Ashes

My life had ended or so I thought:
the years invested, the pain it brought.
Curled on the floor a withering wreck,
no dignity left - but what the heck.

Pleading and begging for him to stay,
what else could I do but sit and pray?
Hope for a miracle that would change his mind -
see that I was loving and gentle and kind.

My mother had said, "You make your bed",
and here I was living, but totally dead.
The physical pain I learnt to endure,
but for the pain in my heart there wasn't a cure.

I tried my best to make him happy,
but what ever I did, he said it was *crappy*.
I cooked and I cleaned to within an inch of my life,
but in return he just took a knife:

waving and screaming and calling me *fat*.
Was this the same man that promised me that
if I honoured, obeyed and served him okay,
a princess I'd be till the end of the day?

"Where has the charmer in uniform gone?"
- a question I asked, but not for too long.
To question or quiz this man in my life
would only result in trouble and strife.

I had only asked why he was late,
and before I knew it, it had signed my fate.

There I was lying battered and bruised,
and the man of my dreams calling me *a fool*.

I'm ugly and useless and not worth the fight.
He' s leaving me now - try as I might
my life has ended as he walks out the door…

I wish I was dead and living no more.

Jacqui

The Note

Time will pass, wounds will heal and pain will go, but good memories will live on. When people think of me, if you do, smile. I am at peace, all the pain and hurt have gone. I will be watching down on you all, so watch out you might find me sitting at the bottom of your bed and you don't want that. Nor do I never know what you're going to be doing.

We all have goals in life and I couldn't make mine or control mine but this one I can. Sally must know nothing until the end. All I wanted was to be with Sally and be happy. Baby I am so sorry. You have Jake, soon he will give you more love than you can ever imagine. Stop colouring your hair and become a grey hair granny. Don't spoil him just give him love and you have plenty of that to give.

I love you so much, I am sorry baby for hurting you, be happy. I will now be able to see some of my friends. Baby I love you so much please forgive me, Forgive me baby I couldn't get up this time, baby smile when you think of me. I'll be watching over you, be happy, remember the song 'better love changes', mine never did baby. Goodbye darling, be happy forever in my heart.

Angie

How Did It Ever Come To This?

The Marriage
Is it really 20 years, this mental hell? How could I possibly
know outside my bubble of marrying my childhood
sweetheart that our family could face so many traumas?
How ludicrous to think the grass could be greener on the
other side.

Together with my husband 17 years, we had our ups and
downs. Had a lovely home, three gorgeous boys, a lovely
family. All 'normal'. Was it just that that made me think
'Surely there's something better out there'? Was it a mid-
life crisis, my wish to be a teen again? Itchy feet, a whim?

No one said it would last; he was 18, I was 16 and at college.
He was a 'bad boy', opposites attract. He on probation,
about to go inside; me training to be a medical secretary. He
smoked dope, was a fighter; me an arty airy-fairy hippy,
peace and love. He attracted all the loud girls, the rough
tomboys, the bikers. He had long red hair, a long red beard,
they called him Daisy. I scratched his name on my arm. I
was besotted. The boring boyfriend I had was so tame. We
fell in love. I stopped him going to prison.

Married at 18 and 20 years. Got a house by 25; we had 3
lovely boys, the last one being a red head; of course, he
joked and said the others were the milkman's. I was the
perfect mum, perfect wife as it were. His family were my
family, vice versa. He was a builder, had tattoos, a charmer.
He took me to Paris, to Holland and Belgium. He drank and
smoked, I didn't. My sons were doing well at school, very
bright. His mates came round, we used to flirt. I loved him.

I'll never know to this day what went wrong. I had a brainstorm when I just said I'd had enough. What was it?

We can't change or turn clocks back. I wanted a divorce; thought I could be independent. Do it alone, bring up the boys alone. Get shot of him, find myself, be more than a 'Mum'. He was devastated, the boys were dumbfounded. He went, didn't put up a fight. Within 5 months we were divorced.

The Aftermath
Lo and behold by the seventh month he had moved in with a barmaid, her younger (than me), no kids. He had been having a fling for years. The tables turned. He never drove while we were together. We walked everywhere, even the kids. Now he learned to drive, became a lorry driver. Paid nothing for my sons, disowned them. God, it wasn't their fault.

Now we had a dysfunctional family. A 17 year old who turned to drugs and a 14 year old who unbeknown to anyone self-harmed, a 10 year old who was the apple of her Daddy's eye who quickly became a pawn in a very ugly game.

Our bubble was burst. My nightmare only beginning. I was 34 but naïve, looking 18 so I was told; I changed my image, became more outgoing, started a college course, felt strong. Found some female friends, was going to learn to drive. He found love, so could I! There was so much to look forward to for all of us.

Two years down the line I was nursing my Mum and Dad, both with cancer. My Mum had a fall, my Dad in a London hospital. It was the horror of finding my Mum dead and having to break the news to my Dad that was the trigger that started my binge drinking. Still I smiled. We found a flat for my Dad, I nursed him every day, did his shopping. The boys were finding their feet.

I didn't have time to find love, I had enough on my plate. Always had a smile, always dancing in my kitchen, waving to people as they went past. My sons were my friends, we laughed as they went through different phases. I went out Fridays to let my hair down. They were my world. Five years passed by, I was studying, went through all the religions; nah, that weren't for me.

I wanted somewhere my son could go with his mates, I could socialise, meet people. We joined a club. We had fun; my babe was 13 and had his mates. I was still studying, wanted to better myself. My ex had been sterilised and I was told I could have no kids any more. I wasn't thinking of relationships at all. Went to a Medium for a laugh; she said you are going to have a child at 38 and your life will be in danger; there will be police involved, an injunction, and you will always have two men fighting over you. I laughed, it was insane, I was at my happiest.

The Stalker
The social club was somewhere to go with our kids. Me and friends used to have cheap drinks and then go into town. My happiness was soon to be destroyed. I didn't take much notice of the biker in the leather jacket at the club but I felt him watching me. He wasn't my type and probably nearer my older son's age, about 21 or 22. Drove a huge purple motorbike, struck me as a weirdo.

For a while I would see the bike going past my house, sometimes see him in a little blue car. Unbeknown to me I had a stalker. The nightmare had begun, my life soon to change forever. The pain and torture soon to begin. My mind still now trying to block out the pain. Dear God, why me? Why did I go to that silly club, cheap drinks, God how they cost me. The bright, bubbly, singing, dancing, happy go lucky confident girl was gradually going to be eradicated. Why did I decide to even contemplate, let alone allow, that idiot walk with me? I was drunk, stumbling; 'Hang on, this is

not the way to my house'. He took me to garages, I laughed 'You're just being a boy. I don't fancy you, I need to go home'.

He slammed me against a wall. I was too scared, he got my wrist and tried to break it cos I had rejected him. 'If you tell anyone I'll kill you'. I kept quiet. I ran in, went to bed and woke up, my wrist throbbing. If I told my sons they would get put away. I kept quiet. Went to the club as usual. He watched me chat to men and women. He scared me. Over the course of a year, any opportunity, he would hurt me. Said he would kill me and my sons. I kept quiet. It got worse, he got me in some woods and forced me to have sex. Fear stopped me telling. I lost weight, hardly spoke to people; they thought it was because my Dad was dying. Dear God, I was in a horror movie, the injuries got worse. I was throwing up, no surely not. I did a test, oh my God I was pregnant; oh my God, the immaculate conception. I had no boyfriend, how could I explain this to my family. I was 38 and I was pregnant. I hid it, wore baggy jumpers. Not only was I hiding the weekly abuse, I was hiding a baby. Who could I tell? I told a friend I had a one night stand. I went to hospital but they said I was too far gone to abort.

I stopped going where he was, started preparing for a baby, nearly lost him at 22 weeks, he was poorly inside me. I had to tell my Dad; he was shocked but said 'you'll get through it'.

My sons were horrified; not only was there going to be a new baby but they didn't know who the father was. My babe said 'Get rid of it Mum'. The baby came on February 20th, Pancake Day. He was very ill and taken into special care. My sister-in-law was at the birth; she couldn't have children, she talked of adopting him. This poor little baby; I bonded with him, he was gorgeous, my own Dad held him, my sons and their friends held him. How could anyone hurt him?

The Abuser

The horror hadn't even begun for both of us. The abuser got wind I'd had the baby. Deep down he knew it was his. His first child a little boy. He kept circling the house; he turned up; could he see his son? How the hell could I explain to anyone that this monster at the door was my baby's Dad? I was in such a dilemma; perhaps he had a heart, dear dear God, why did I let him in? The horror was surreal. My head was telling me to protect my baby, protect my sons. The truth was I was my Dad's carer; I was getting money to look after him. The bastard didn't want to bond with his son at all; he wanted my money for his gambling. Once in the house he frogmarched me upstairs and that's where we lived for a year. To cut a long story short he raped me everyday for a year. No kisses, no cuddles, pinned my arms back and told me not to scream. My baby was thrown in the cot when his first word was Dadda; he said 'Shut up you little bastard'. We were all in danger. He isolated me from everyone. I missed the last year of my Dad's life; he lost the first year of his new grandson.

I tried to escape his control but was too weak. I only whispered, didn't want to talk to anyone. I had a dislocated shoulder, even a broken leg; I had to say I fell. He said 'Shut the fuck up, grizzling'. I was in agony. Literally at death's door and with a very disturbed little baby. He raped me in front of him every day.

The Final Ordeal
I phoned a doctor and whispered 'Please help me'. He was arrested, put on bail, broke every bail to rape me. He got put on remand. I went in a refuge. When I came back for Christmas with my sons, who were now on bail themselves for going to smash up his bike and parent's home because they couldn't protect me, little did I know they had let him home for Christmas.

My baby was with a friend and I was going to meet my sons in town for a drink. I went to the station hotel for a drink and went to the toilet. He was there. I knew I was in for it.

I couldn't scream, I froze, he dragged me through the park nearby, ripped my clothes. I tried so hard to get him off. It was an hour long ordeal; my phone was ringing but he had it. He said, 'I'm gonna kill you, then your family'. It was a freezing Xmas eve, and I remember thinking 'This is it, I'm going to die. What ever have I done to this awful man to make him hate me so much?' He knocked me down so hard I banged my head. I remember thinking 'Not like this, I don't want to die like this'. I played dead, thinking he would go. He stripped me naked, I was so cold. He tried to rape me but he couldn't get aroused so he got a bit of branch

and rammed it in me. I was crying, then he pulled me up. I
tried to get something on. I remember hearing a voice 'Run
for your life'. I ran, my head hurt so much; he'd fractured
my skull, my clothes were in shreds. I ran, I heard him
shouting I'm going to kill your baby and your sons. I banged
on my friend's door; she opened it; I fell in and she phoned
the police.

My Life Sentence
I woke up in hospital, it was Xmas Day. He was arrested for
rape. He only did 9 months in prison; I've got a life
sentence. Some days I wish he had killed me because I'll
never know what I did to be violated so much.

Fourteen years down the line I'm still a zombie. Drink,
pills, nothing blocks out the pain. My poor sons lost 'their
Mum' years ago. I'm an empty Shell. I'm 53 and can't
function. How can I love if I don't love myself? I don't
want to grow old
alone, bitter and twisted. I want to move on from my
torment.

You can heal a broken leg but it's hard to heal a broken spirit
and crushed soul. It's easier to stay away, hide away, than
confront your fears. Everyday my only sanctuary is to soak
in the bath but it lasts hours. Scrub away the dirt, the pain,
the shame.

Can't find the right clothes to wear. Years have gone by but
I can't wear a skirt. 'Oh, it's her fault, she opened her legs'.
'It's her fault she dropped her kacks'. 'The way she dressed,
she asked for it'.

I hear this voice every day 'I don't want to be here any more. Everyone would be better off without me'. I didn't want to be in this mess, my life's a mess, my head's a mess. No job, no money, can't trust, feel useless. Nothing makes sense in this muddled head. Limbo and purgatory. Wish it would end. Why don't people believe me when I say I've lost the plot?

Gina

Numb

I don't want drugs no more
I want to be free from pain
I don't want to have to put
Heroin through my veins

But how else can I cope
In my world that is so dark
I want to be free and happy
Like a child in the park

But another night is coming
I know just what's in store
The late news has just finished
So he'll walk through the door

I dash into the bathroom
To numb myself again
This is for his pleasure
The rules that make his game

I feel the heroin flow
Numbing each open sore
It's the only way I know
When I've got be his whore

I feel his breath, all smelly
And smothering my face
I feel sick to the stomach
As I'm forced to get his taste

At last it's over

Well for now anyway
It will soon be light
Oh no, another day

Claire

Worthless   Ugly   Bitch   Stupid Cow
Drop Dead   Waste of Space   Tart

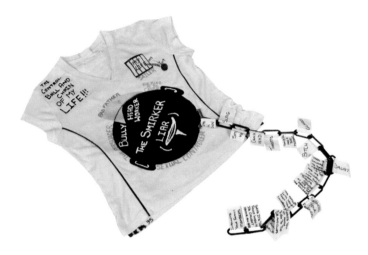

The control ball and chain of my life!!!

To Be Free...

Dark is the way, I have trod
Eager to please, eager to nod.
Dark is the place on this map
Where I am, and how to get back.

Bruises blue, faces pale, shock and anger
I cry and wail!
Heavy are the bags in hand and strain
Inside emptiness, alone and pain
Heavy is the heart in my chest.
Heavy is my soul seeking rest.

Light is the way, through hope and chance,
A helping hand and an outstretched arm,
My soul will rise, sing and dance
I shall be safe, my children calm.
No more pain, and no more harm.

Hannah

The Water Of Life

Water is vital for life, without it nothing can exist. That was what my husband was to me. He was like water. I couldn't survive without him but, just as water gives life, it can take it away. He completely surrounded me so that I was drowning in him. I couldn't breathe. Someone that had been so soft and gentle like a trickling stream became angry and dangerous like a ferocious waterfall.

To the outside world I had it all, people often said how lucky I was. I had a lovely big house, 2 wonderful children and a handsome charming husband. What they didn't realise was that, when they weren't looking, that charming husband of mine became a monster. I would smile at them and agree ' yes I am very lucky', but inside I was dead.

I had fallen into a dark well and I couldn't get out. I wanted someone to rescue me but no one even knew I was there. I would walk around seemingly happy and care free but inside I was screaming. I felt trapped and I couldn't find the door to get out. Have you ever looked in the mirror and not recognised your own reflection? I have, I've stood gazing at myself and asked, Who are you? What have you done with Anna? Where did she go?

I try to remember the beginning, I was so naïve. I had met this wonderful man, he was so caring and thoughtful, sensitive, so funny and loving, so perfect. Too good to be true - quite literally!! I had never been loved like that before. It seemed like he just wanted to protect me, checking if I was ok; he was always worrying about me, and I felt safe.

Once we were married and living together it all became more intense. He said he would take care of all the financial matters because he didn't want me to be stressed over it. He said I already worked hard enough and he wanted to help me, make life easier for me. He would take me to and from work. He would call to check I arrived safely every morning. He would also ring in the day to see if I was busy and I would have to ring to let him know I was leaving. He said he didn't want to share me with anyone. We didn't really go out and we didn't have anyone over much either.

I had moved away from my home town when we got married and so I was isolated from my family and friends; it just meant that I needed him more. He was everything to me and I just wanted to please him and yet sometimes I would get it wrong. He was quick to lose his temper but it would blow over, until the next time.

I became depressed but didn't accept it. I couldn't see why I would be because, just as I was pretending to everyone else that all was ok, I was also lying to myself. But deep down I knew and I thought it was my fault.

Once our boys arrived, life got progressively worse. On one hand I had everything I wanted - I had always dreamed of having a family and I had it. Even though my sons gave me more joy than I could ever have hoped for, I became more trapped. What I had initially thought was a protective caring person was in fact someone who needed to take over everything about me. He controlled everything. I couldn't even go to the toilet at home without telling him. I was constantly trying to work out what he wanted me to say and what he wanted me to do. How he wanted me to be.

I lost myself.

I was trapped in my own body. I forgot what I liked, I couldn't remember what I wanted, I didn't know who I was.

Until one day it just all got too much. I reached a point where it was sink or swim. I went looking for help. I saw the doctor, the councillor, the police, the social worker, the solicitor, then I found Women's Aid. I've decided I'm not going to drown in him. I'm learning to swim and I'm heading for the shore.

Anna

Please

I have waited for so long
To leave this nightmare
So I pick up the phone
Only to be told
There are no spaces in the refuge
The situation is getting worse

I am walking on eggshells
Not sure what will happen next
All I want to do
Is break down and cry
Please let there be a breakthrough

Emma

PART II
The Breakthrough

Life in a Refuge

The Lead Up
I am about to go into the Refuge
I have five more days to go
I am scared and I am frightened
But I know this is what I must do
I must deal with the path my life has taken as best I can
I have to be strong for my daughter's sake and do what's best
for both of us
But inside I am shaking and still in shock
It is the unknown that scares me
I don't know what to expect
But I have to take this chance and make the most of this
opportunity

Arrival
Well, at last I am here
I never thought I was strong enough to do this
I've come here with nothing. I am in clothes that never
should be put together – a yellow cardie, green top and pink
bottoms
But they are clean and I am so grateful for them
I don't know what to expect but for the first time in ages I
feel safe and I feel cared for

Anger and Reflection
How have I come to this point in my life?
How the hell did I get here?
I am sitting in a warm sunny garden; everything is calm
and peaceful.
How can that be when it feels like everything in my world is
collapsing around me?

It should be pouring with rain, with thunder and lightening.

I am living in a refuge. A bloody refuge of all places
Somewhere that I never thought I'd be
How has my life come to this?

Coming to Terms
Well, I've been here for five weeks now
And it feels like a lifetime
I fought tooth and nail not to come here
But, you know, I think that it's the best thing that I've ever done.
Nobody ever wants to come into a Refuge, there is a stigma attached to them. I don't know why.
Everyone is here for very different reasons. It can be for anything.
It doesn't have to be for domestic violence or physical abuse.
It is for those who are being controlled or bullied, being put down by their partner or family.
But we are all here for the same reason: we want to find ourselves again, find the person we used to be.
We want to change our lives for our children's sake.
To find strength again.
To show the men that we can cope without them, and we can do a great job too.

Thank you
I need to give thanks for what I have gained
For when I came to Women's Aid I was lost, I was hurt.
I felt as if my life was falling away from me and there was nothing I could do to stop it
I'd been hurt by a man I loved and trusted. I had nowhere to turn and no-one to talk to.

Then I came here. And I felt like a light had been switched on.
People understood and they were kind.

I didn't feel so alone. People smiled at me and made me feel welcome.
Things are still hard but with this amount of support things are getting easier.
I feel that I am slowly finding myself again.
It's such a great thing they do. They help so many people,
They are in the background, quietly going on, most people don't know that they are there. I never did.
But without them so many women and children would not be alive.

Annie

Déjà Vu

How d' fuck did I end up here?
Back in refuge after less than a year
Back with people I don't even know
And to make shit worse it's started to snow

My room is a cell and I'm in a bunk bed
But I gotta stick it out and follow my head
Yet I'm so in love that I just wanna cry
But my pride gotta win, gotta hold my head high

Coz my babies deserve the best that there is
And that's what they'll get if I stick at this
They're depending on me to make shit right
It's time for me and my heart to fight

Coz even though refuge is fucking crap
At least I got my bears sitting here on my lap
I gotta move on, fix up and make a home
That me and my little ones can call our own
Where everything's organised, tidy and clean
And his ten ton of shit ain't nowhere to be seen
Let him get his own place stand on his own two feet
Sort out his own shit so he and the kids can meet

He can have his place and I can have mine
Coz as long as my bears are happy I'll be fine
Jesus have mercy and guide me through
Give me the strength to do what I gotta do

Every night I pray it's gonna be alright
Ask my God to help and show me the light

Why can't I have a happy ever after
I've put in the work always been a grafter

All I've ever wanted was a happy family
but now I understand what will be will be

Anon

'Til the Line Snapped

Like a fisherman he would cast out his line. His bait would
be the threat of committing suicide or he'd say he had
changed, that he loved me and was suddenly caring again. Or
he'd make me feel guilty about how it affected our children;
sometimes he would just threaten to take them away. And so
I would bite every time like an unsuspecting fish. And he'd
reel me in. For a short while he'd be nice, loving even. But
once he had me, once I was caught, I was like a fish out of
water. Helpless and barely alive. His mood would change
and I couldn't swim away.

I was hooked!

It's easy for someone else, someone who's never loved
someone who abuses them physically or mentally, to say
"why didn't you just leave?" "Why did you let this happen
to you?" But it's not as easy as that. You think you deserve
it. Unknowingly you've been brainwashed into thinking that.
You also love him. So you live in hope that one day it'll all be
fine. You build your life on those few moments when he's in
a good mood and the water is calm. For me, when he looked
at me and smiled and spoke nicely to me because, for
whatever reason, he was in a happy mood, I felt like it was
the sun shining on my face. It was always short lived and he
was soon tempestuous again and I was back in the cold. But
that just made those few moments when he was in a good
mood even more precious. So, I would long for it again, I'd
wait around for it again. Do anything I could to please him
until eventually I'd run out of energy. That's when I'd start
slipping from his grasp. You get to a point where you can't
take it any more; you're worn out. You don't care what

happens, you just know that you can't live like that any more.

I'd turn away. That's when he'd start being nice and I would feel myself being reeled back in.

I don't know how many times we went through this cycle, too many to count. And with each time it got worse. I was getting help from counselling and women's aid, so I was getting stronger. I knew I wanted a better life for myself and my children. But as I found more courage, he had to strengthen his tactics to scare me into being caught again. Until eventually I gained some respect for myself and in doing that I saw him for what he was. I guess I stopped being in love with him and so the line snapped.

Anna

A Hard Question

Someone asked me today why I didn't like myself and what I didn't like about myself.

I found that question so hard to answer; which surprises me.

I suppose I hate myself for going out with my ex because of what he did, not only to me but also my daughter. She saw and heard things that she should never have been party to. And it's stayed with her, frightened her.

I blame myself for losing my daughter, who would have been three years old now, even though there was nothing that I could have done. It wasn't my fault that she died but I blame myself. It eats me up.

I blame myself for what my Grandad did to me when I was 12 years old.

I don't like the fact that I try to make everyone else happy but never try to make myself happy. I get taken advantage of sometimes, perhaps I'm too giving.

I don't say what I mean or really want to say. I say things that I think people want to hear instead of telling them exactly how I feel.

I feel hurt by family and their lack of support.

I feel lost.

I feel alone

Annie
46

Day By Day

Every morning come sunshine or rain
I put on my mask to hide my pain
The foundation on my life is dull and fake
And my mascara hides how much my eyes ache

It's a punishment to even open my eyes
And it seems that no one hears me cry
My babies are my guiding star, shining bright
But I dread the moment when I kiss them goodnight

Coz then I lie in bed alone and afraid
But not of the dark just of the next day
I'm losing my religion my faith and my prayer
And if that makes me evil then I really don't care

Coz I'm sick of being who I wasn't born to be
I'm stuck behind this mask for no one to see
Trapped in a cage of depression and strain
Finally broke free yet still I feel pain

Constantly talking just to stop the silence
Now who should I turn to when I need guidance?
I've prayed and I've cried even dropped to my knees
So if Jesus loves me where the fuck's he?

When did I become so bitter and mad?
When did I last wake up not sad?
Why after everything that you put me through
Am I still so deeply in love with you?

I gotta fix up and face up to things
Life ain't about roses or diamond rings
I'm gonna die one day sad and lonely
But in the mean time I just need to be me

I'm gonna choose what clothes I wear
And I'm gonna choose how I want my hair
You'll always have my heart but you've killed it dead
So these are the last tears I'm gonna shed

I'm gonna be strong coz my babies need me
I'll hold my head up high and enjoy being free
Wipe away tears, lock my feelings away
Spark up a fag and live day by day.

Anon

Innocent.
I only cried.

He exploded leaving me paralysed.
Mum didn't escape.

The Revelation

When I first came to the refuge, full to the brim with depression and oppression from an inhumane partner I was already at my lowest point. But then came another complete bombshell to cope with. I had been sexually abused by a male neighbour as a child of three.

I used to wander round their house as a child with a dolly his wife had knitted for me, called Sandy, made of wool. She would cuddle me and make a fuss of me because she had lots of boys but no girls.

Unbeknown to her he would take me to the pigeon shed at the bottom of the garden on the pretext of showing me the baby pigeons. But he had another sinister reason, he would put a baby pigeon in my hands and tell me not to drop it while his fingers found me down there and hurt me, all the while telling me not to drop the baby bird. He used my love for birds and all animals against me to get his own gratification. What a sick bastard, I was three for Christ sake!

This on top of a stressful childhood was all too much to bear. Now I am trying to come to terms with my life as shit as it has been. I am getting there and still feel there is a path of good, I must climb out of these depths of despair. I am shaking as I look at the words on these pages. Is it with anger? Hopefully later with contempt, for all the people who have put a dark black shadow over my life. I am now walking more into the light and finding things I enjoy doing, which I should have enjoyed as a child - reading, painting, tennis, learning, play. I feel like a three year old who missed out on life. No encouragement. No love. No Care.

I was fifty at five, perhaps that's why I feel such a child now but it's too late to go back and grow up again. Now I will pursue my future for all the things I should have done as a child, and be the strong thoughtful person I should have been. That's where my partner never understood about life. You do not give to receive, you give because you enjoy it. If women ruled the world there would be no wars.

The nearly new Laura

Mothers and Fathers

Look after your children well and protect
Even when you know you're right and others may object

Give the most important thing, your love and your time
Don't say no when they ask you to read that nursery rhyme

To cherish and encourage their growing talent
Don't let them harbour thoughts of being not good enough
in torment

Enjoy their childhood with them and let them grow
These are the people of the future we sow.

Laura

Ode To Auntie Jean

My Auntie Jean died when she was eighty. What a strong lovely lady she was, my dad's sister. Born in Hollywood, Ireland, Yes Hollywood. My granddad came to England when his children were little - Jean, Babs, Kenneth, and Billy. My dad, Billy, joined the Navy and went to war. Jean worked in a factory in Ipswich and met a man, married and had five children.

Those days you put up and shut up. Her husband was violent and abusive but in those days you did not run. My Auntie was strong after all the beatings. She wanted to protect her children. The police were called to her home several times but then they had no power, no refuges existed. Eventually she fled to Nottingham with the kids and worked hard to keep them safe.

My Auntie, my rock. At the funeral there were my cousins, all fine strong pillars of the community - a policeman, a doctor. One lives in Spain, Susan lives in America and her children teach.

My brave, courageous Auntie I love you to bits. It was your strength that inspired me when I was at my lowest ebb. R.I.P

Anon

Let Her Down

I feel as if I've really let my daughter down. I've gone from one prison to another as if we haven't gone through enough hell.

I left my partner just before Christmas and I loved him more than anything in the world. In the past I had trouble with commitment so this time I was determined to make it work so I really stayed much longer than I should have. In the end I had to make it end for the sake of my child.

My partner was my world - I feel as if he destroyed me. I don't recognise myself any more. Also he knew that I didn't get on with my parents and living with them now, it feels as if he is still winning. I managed to get away and he is still controlling me.

It feels strange being allowed to go out on my own, and to eat what I want to. But now I have gone to the other extreme and I don't eat. It feels as if it's the only thing that I can control in my life! I feel as though I have drawn into myself and find it hard mixing with people. I need help. I feel as if I am plodding along. I can't cope any more and the only thing that keeps me going is my daughter. But for how much longer will I feel like that?

I am lying in my bed in the smallest room, listening to my parents fighting downstairs. They are getting everything ready for my brother to come back. He's only coming back for a few days, anyone would think that royalty's coming. Does he realise how much they are doing for him? Does he realise how hard it is for me? I am told when I am allowed to get up, what time to get home, I have to eat dinner with them, but told what to cook for my daughter. I have to put her to bed when they think that the time is right.

My mother can't accept that I'm the mother now. I keep being told that it is their house and I have to follow their rules. I am in prison all over again.

I am so scared to break free for I know how they would react. I don't want to lose my daughter and I am scared that they will take her away from me. My mum has told me that they had a family meeting before and discussed it.

I am 32 years old, but I feel 15.

Annie

I never got this big.
He killed me.

Can I have my heart back?

A New Found Hope

A holiday, my brother and I, a telephone call, and anxious
cry,
So we have travelled through the night, looking for a place to
hide.

My friend, my soulmate, my happiness he waits,
"When, when will I see her again"
I'll see him soon, each minute love grows,
A few more weeks, and we both will know.

Not knowing how to let it out, I cut, and cut, in a way
It helped. I promise my mum, never again, but future
Will tell, only then.

Now not knowing how to express myself, my six string my
Voice, it's a cry for help, the words I write, songs of love
And peace, what I want this world to be.

Safe in my room, safe from him, outside my walls this
World is grim, study, study, art and song, to keep myself
Busy all day long.

Poke, poke, on my head, venom in his words, hate in
His head, a lonely man, angry at the world...
Alcohol on his breath, a finger curled.

Work, study, work, try my best for an easy life,
Falling, falling, I backslide.
Through no fault of my own, or the ones before, but life
Is cruel, it makes you numb, tired and sore.

I know my day will come, when I'll look back, and say,
"Look how far I've come, here I wish to stay",
My tears are here to remind me, and others all around me,
Even the happiest person can get angry and lonely.

So far from home, and everything I knew,
I wake every night crying and screaming,
Hope is near, and until my day,
I stay strong, yes, strong I will stay,

Over the bridge, when I see the hills
We are home! We are home!

Danielle (just 16 years old)

It's Not Me!

As autumn approached and the nights drew in, one of the
"rules" I had to follow was to have the curtains drawn before
he got home. Sounds simple, doesn't it? But don't be fooled
by the simplicity of it. Because every evening when he
arrived home and checked them, he would always, without
fail, angrily comment that I hadn't closed them properly. It
was one of many things that I always seemed to get wrong. I
felt useless and inadequate about everything. He would
always have to re-do the curtains. I used to watch him
attentively, trying to see what he was doing differently and
every evening I would try and replicate how he did them. I
even tried to copy the movement of his hand. The way he
smoothed the edge of the curtain with a short sharp action
using the back of his hand. The right curtain had to overlap
the left, but only just slightly. I would stand back as he did,
to get full view of my efforts. To me it looked the same but
his eyes always found a fault.

Then one morning I decided I wouldn't open them. My son
and I spent the whole day with all the curtains in the house
drawn. I thought it would be one thing off the list of "rules"
that would be right that evening.
He came home.
He checked the curtains.
He began to shout.
He said they weren't closed properly.

That's when I first realised: it's not me!

It doesn't matter how perfectly I draw the curtains or how I do anything else, I'm never going to get it right in his eyes. Whatever I do, it's never going to be good enough for him.

I'd like to say everything changed that day, but it didn't. I still often blamed myself and I still lived like that, trying to do everything "right" for many more years. But a little light got turned on inside me that evening as I looked at those curtains and with time it grew into what is now a burning flame. Today I'm not living that impossible life and I now know.

It's not me!

Anna

Your Problems

I know that you have problems
But they're not excuses!
We all have problems
You have a drink problem and a serious anger problem

You need to take stock
Think about them
Stop trying to forget about them

And please, for me, don't go out with anyone else, especially
someone with children.

Please don't put them through what you put me through.
It's not fair

And please, stop blaming me! I didn't do anything for God's
sake!
I didn't

Annie

Once Upon a time...

Today I went to a solicitor to swear an oath to a statement in regard to divorcing my husband. At first I felt silly, reaching out my hand to touch the white bible which the solicitor held. And so I giggled. Then, he said "repeat after me" and I had to repeat my full name and declare I wanted to divorce my husband, using his full name. I had a flash back to our wedding day. I had giggled on that day too as I began saying our vows. I had repeated after the priest and declared that I would love my husband, for better or for worse, till death do us part. And here I was undoing it. I was overwhelmed by great sadness. I struggled to retain my emotions. Tears welled in my eyes but did not fall and I had to pause a moment to stop my voice from squeaking.

A pain still shoots in my heart as I think of it and I'm not fully sure why. I should be elated. I'm one step closer to being free from a bully. But I don't want to be divorced. It's against my beliefs. And I don't mean the religious ones, I mean my own. I saw marriage as forever. So, I guess I'm upset for a shattered dream. But that's all it was, a dream.

When I was little, one of my favourite stories was Cinderella. Like most little girls, I dreamt of finding my own handsome prince, getting married, having a family and living happily ever after! I'm ashamed now to admit, that subconsciously I had a check list and my husband, when I met him, ticked every single box. He was a fairytale, a dream come true? Unfortunately not. The reality of marriage was a nightmare. The prince I kissed turned into a toad. Illusion never became something real. Once upon a

64

time.... didn't have a happily ever after, but it's not the end of the story. It's just the end of a chapter.

Anna

PART III
The Beginning

It Doesn't Matter

It doesn't matter if I don't want to
Just smile and carry on
It doesn't matter that you hurt me
It's all part of your con

It doesn't matter that you're old
Your skin is saggy and aged
It doesn't matter that you're horrible
Animals like you should be caged

It doesn't matter that you tricked me
I believed your stories and you lie
It doesn't matter that you must be deaf
For you certainly don't hear my cry

It doesn't matter that I have no one
Well that's what you thought anyway
It doesn't matter, well you're wrong
For today is a new day.

Claire

The difference

He used to
Measure the size
Of carrots cut
Now I can
Cut the carrots
How I want

Now I cut
Things the way
I want
What difference
Does it make
Tastes the same
In the end

But it makes a difference to me

Emma

Alone
Bewildered
Useless
Stressed
Exhausted
Depressed

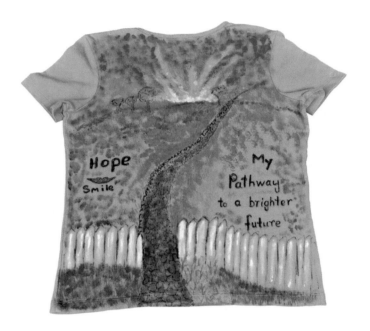

My pathway to a brighter future.

Hope

There is hope.
For one day I know that I will get over this
And all of this will be a bad dream
Life is out there
I am better than that
I didn't deserve what you put me through
But I am still here
And I have got through it
I am stronger than you are

It hit me yesterday, everything that had happened to me and what I went through. I thought to myself, I am still here. I've come through this. I will come through this, a much better and stronger person because of it. I've got to stop thinking about him and how I miss him, and always look for him. I keep thinking about his good side, but then I think, well I hardly saw that. That isn't him. It's time to let go and it's time to move on. I have something that he hasn't got. I have the most wonderful daughter and friends and family and for that I thank God every day.

Annie

Christchurch Park

My mind was confused and crooked
No sleep when I went to bed
The park gave me solitude and peace
And all my life a brand new lease

To sit amongst nature and the trees
Just to sit and listen to the bees
To sort my mind out
Get rid of anger and all the doubt

The park has given me all of this
It will be my major miss
Christchurch Park I will be back one day
Perhaps I will make it next year in early May

Laura

Ipswich

Ipswich has been my major cure
But Norwich has always been my lure
Ipswich has given me confidence to live
And how much pleasure it is to give

I leave Friday morn, I can't wait
Must get packed ready, mustn't be late
The future looks so bright
Now I'm running towards the light

People guided me to the right choices
No need to bully or shout in loud voices

Laura

First Viewing

Today's the day I might just find
A place to call my home
No longer will I be scared and afraid
I'll be glad to be alone

No more watching on TV
Only what he wants to
No more having him tell me
What I can or can't do

I wonder what it will be like
Will it be a flat?
I don't care if its only a studio
Will I be allowed a cat?

There's probably no pets
That's probably the rule
I hope it's a security door
Before the entrance hall

Will it have carpets
That are soft to the touch?
Maybe it will be laminate
Am I expecting too much?

Will the kitchen come with a cooker
A dishwasher or washing machine?
I'm going to love cooking
In my kitchen that I can clean

Will my bedroom have cupboards

Or wardrobes built in?
Will I have a double bed
Or it may be just a twin?

Either way it will be mine
I'll be the one in charge
No one to shout or demand
Giving it the large

I'll be able to sleep
With no one able to touch me
I can let go of the covers
And they can hang free

I'll be able to lock my own front door
Knowing I'm the only one with a key for sure
At last a safe place I can call my home
I'll be free and at peace, safe, alone

Claire

Happiness

I've had a magical day
My heart and stomach are all over the place
I don't know if what I am feeling is real

I think I am going to take things as they come
See what comes of it

He makes me laugh
When we are sharing lots of jokes
Or tickling each other

Once again I am smiling from ear to ear.

Emma

My Hero

Tim makes me smile
He makes my life worthwhile
When I am sad, Tim knows that I am sad and tries to make
me happy.
We talk and laugh, and watch TV and listen to music
together.
We find the time to listen to each other about our problems.
Life without my friend Tim would be the worst thing for
me!
Because Tim saved me from all the nasty and bad things that
were done to me.
Tim understands life because he cared for his late wife for
over 10 years. She used to be a District Nurse.
Tim helps people with their computer problems and he also
does charity work.
He plays his barrel organ, and is also a Music Arranger
having over 50 tunes published.
Tim is my hero.

Lucy (emerging from the pain and problems)

Phoenix

Many years have passed and how life has changed!
I could never have envisaged my life as it came,
working with women that suffer the pain
from a man they love and a life with no gain.

Confident, happy and full of life:
is this the same woman slashed with a knife?
Gone is the mouse, all timid and shy...

Welcome the woman that can reach for the sky!

The lessons I've learned and the hope that I share,
the message is clear (so please, no fear):
your life doesn't end when you walk out the door,
it just opens a life with so much more.

You can learn to smile and be really happy,
(forget the life that was really crappy),
choose your path, your clothes and your friends,
see the beautiful life that has no end.

Jacqui

I am the dove, black and cold. Trapped in a my cage by the lock of lies.
I cannot move, I cannot take flight for fear of reprisal if I might!
But wait, the lock of lies begins to rust and fall, do I dare take flight?
I make a choice, I make it right, I take a small jump, spread my wings
and fly into the Light.
No longer am I black and cold, I am more me,
I turn white and fly out of the darkness into the light.

I have freedom. This is right.
Linda

Safe as houses?

Don't turn a blind eye

Why?

Why do people not help each other out more?

Why do you close your ears to your next door neighbours' fighting?

And pretend that you cannot hear the boyfriend battering his girlfriend, through the wall?

Every night she takes it!

All she needs is one person to do something

Why are people so afraid to help?

What gets her through is the thought of her children and the small glimmer of hope that all this will end!

Katy

Journey

I found myself quivering in a dark pit and I dragged myself
out of it. And here I am. I'm not going to lie to you. It hasn't
been easy. But it's a well known fact that sometimes things
have to get worse before they get better. And my journey
isn't over yet. But the bruises have faded, the mental scars
are healing and now that I can give myself some worth, my
confidence, self esteem and self belief are all on the up. I'm
34 years old and I feel like life is just beginning!

I wouldn't have got here however, had it not been for the
guidance of Women's Aid. To begin with, it took me a long
while to believe I needed their help. I refused to admit "I
suffer domestic violence". I was very concerned that I would
be wasting their time or worse still, that I would be taking
up the place of someone who really needed it. So, I started
by going along to the Art group. I had no expectations, but
painting feelings on a T-shirt helped me to begin opening up.

The freedom programme was a great help. It was hard at
first because it was a shock to finally see how bad my life
was. No hiding or pretending. But it also made me realise
that what I was going through wasn't acceptable, that it
wasn't my fault and I wasn't alone. As well as having the
encouragement from the leaders I also met other women
who understood what I was going through. We were all on
the same journey.

Being involved in writing this book has been an enormous
help too. I just stumbled on the class one day quite by
accident and I'm so thankful that I did. Writing feelings
down and sharing them in the group (some of which are

printed in this book) helped me to accept what has happened and has helped me to move on further. Friendships have been made too.

I hope, just as writing this book has helped us, that it also helps you who are reading it. Maybe you're reading this out of curiosity, so I hope it has opened your eyes or maybe you're a frightened woman just as I was. I hope this gives you the strength to come on the journey with us.

You are not alone.

Anna

What a pleasure to meet you all!

To all the ladies connected with the violence and abuse of
children and women

What a pleasure to meet you all!

We all arrive with our souls torn apart
Looking for someone to just listen and have a heart

You all do such a fantastic job, we all leave lifted
Even me, I came away really believing I am gifted

To anyone feeling battered, torn and let down
There is great help on the outskirts of Ipswich Town

Laura

THE POETS

Julie has started a new job. She and her sons are happy and life is better ☺ !

Anna has discovered who she is and is making plans for her life and her children. Life is worth living.

Paula is getting stronger in baby steps.

Katy is living happily with her daughter. At the moment she's renovating her new house.

Angie found solace in being able to express her true feelings.

Gina is much stronger and will put up with no more abuse. She is so much happier.

Claire enjoys drama and spends a lot of her time involved in her community. She's now got her own place.

Hannah spent some time in refuge.

Laura has enrolled on a Creative Writing course because she loves to write. She lives with her cat and no-one tells her what to do any more.

Danielle also spent some time in refuge.

Emma has developed a love of arts and crafts, and has made lasting friendships from being involved with the Women Write group.

Lucy feels like she can finally talk about what happened.

Linda is still enjoying amateur painting. She'd like to take it up professionally one day.

Jacqui survived and is now trying to give back to others for the help that she received. She works for Lighthouse Women's Aid.

PASSIONATE ABOUT LOVE, PEACE AND JUSTICE

Men are active in equality struggles in countries and communities thousands of miles away, and that is important, but I see the treating of women as less than equal as the freedom activity that is nearest home. I don't want my women friends to be judged as commodities, as pieces of meat . It demeans them and it demeans me, that women think that "all" men could think like this.

It's time for men to take their share of the responsibility for ending violence against women. As a man recently wrote on our pledge page "Violence will only cease when Men challenge other men , their attitudes and beliefs. If you care for your mother, sister, aunt or any female in your life then join the White Ribbon Campaign and help work to make the world a safer and fairer place".

Imagine a World without Violence against Women - What would it be like ?

The response I've had have included the following.......
Loving, Happy, Peaceful, Safe.......
NORMAL

I want to live in a Normal world

ASK for her opinion
LISTEN her reply
RESPECT her reply

"Wearing a Ribbon is not enough, but it's a good first start"

White Ribbon Campaign is the largest campaign in the world of Men challenging other Men to work towards Ending Violence against Women.

Chris Green Director
White Ribbon Campaign

For more information please go to:-
www.whiteribboncampaign.co.uk

WHERE TO GO FOR HELP

If you are experiencing abuse, you are not alone.
In an emergency, or if you feel in danger, phone **999**
immediately. You can do this from a mobile, even if you
don't have credit.

National Helplines

National Domestic Violence Helpline
0808 2000 247
The 24/7 freephone National DV Helpline can provide
confidential advice for women experiencing domestic abuse,
or others calling on their behalf, from anywhere in the UK.
They can also point you towards domestic abuse
organisations in your area.

Women's Aid
Women's Aid is the key national charity working to end
domestic violence and abuse against women and children.
They co-run the National DV Helpline with Refuge.
www.womensaid.org.uk.

ChildLine
0800 1111
ChildLine is a national counselling service for children and
young people. If you're a young person and you're worried
about something, big or small, you can speak to someone
about it by calling ChildLine.
www.childline.org.uk

NSPCC Helpline
0808 800 5000
If you are an adult and you have concerns about a child, you can get free, confidential advice by calling the NSPCC Helpline, available 24hrs a day.
www.nspcc.org.uk

Rape Crisis
0808 802 9999
Freephone helpline for women and girls who have been raped or sexually assaulted. The helpline is open daily 12 – 2.30pm and 7pm – 9.30pm, for advice and support.
www.rapecrisis.org.uk

Men's Advice Line
0808 801 0327
Providing help and support for male victims of domestic violence. Calls are free. The helpline is open Mon-Fri, 10am – 1pm and 2pm – 5pm.
www.mensadviceline.org.uk

Broken Rainbow
0300 999 5428
Broken Rainbow is the national domestic violence charity for gay, lesbian, bisexual and transgender people, offering advice, support and referral services to LGBT people experiencing homophobic, transphobic and same sex domestic violence.
Helpline is open Mon 2pm – 8pm, Wed 10am – 5pm, Thurs 2pm – 8pm.
www.broken-rainbow.org.uk

Respect
0808 802 4040

Respect runs a confidential helpline for domestic violence perpetrators (male or female). They offer information and advice to support perpetrators stop their violence and change their abusive behaviours.

Helpline is open Mon – Fri, 10am – 1pm and 2pm – 5pm.

www.respectphoneline.org.uk

Suffolk Helplines

Lighthouse Women's Aid

Lighthouse is a registered charity based in Suffolk. We provide advice, support and safe accommodation to women and children who are experiencing or who have experienced domestic abuse. We run the Freedom Programme in Ipswich (www.freedomprogramme.co.uk), a variety of support groups and counselling. Our Independent Domestic Violence Advisors can offer one-to-one support for women going through the justice system and the courts due to domestic abuse.

Head Office 01473 220 776 (for general enquiries)
Helpline 01473 745 111 (for advice)

Our 24hr helpline provides confidential and non-judgemental advice to women, or others calling on their behalf. Between 5pm and 9am, please leave a message and we will call you back within 15mins.

www.lighthousewa.org.uk

The Ferns
0300 123 5058
The Ferns is a SARC (Sexual Assault Referral Centre). They offer medical care and emotional support to any victim of rape and sexual assault. The helpline is 24hrs.

Suffolk Rape Crisis
0800 0850 520
Local support and confidential advice for women who have experienced rape or sexual assault.
Helpline is open Tues and Thurs, 7pm – 9pm.

Domestic Violence in the UK

In the UK:

Domestic violence accounts for 25% of all reported violent crime.

A woman is killed by a violence partner or former partner every 3 days.

It is estimated that 1 in 4 women will experience domestic violence in their lifetime.

A woman is assaulted 35 times on average before she seeks help.

112 women a year are killed by their partners or former partners.

98% of domestic violence charges are withdrawn by the complainant before the case gets to court.

A woman is 30% more likely to be assaulted while she is pregnant.

The police receive a complaint about domestic violence every 60 seconds.

A woman is assaulted in her home every 6 seconds.